Leading up to More

Mandi Kreidler

Presentation by *BookLeaf Publishing*

Web: www.bookleafpub.com

E-mail: info@bookleafpub.com

ISBN: 9789357442343

First edition 2023

Daydreams

Interpret them however you wish

Paint them a picture on your minds door

Whether it be merciless heartbreak or fervent bliss

Discover all of the reasons that lead you to more

Imagination

I remember my childhood paradise
A beach near the terrace
My very first crush
Two real best friends

I remember my first two wheel bike ride
A book bag black eye
A parking lot kiss
The most delicate willow

I remember the worlds we created
Makeshift houses
Extravagant stories
Stairwells of laughter

I remember the hill covered in snow
Dancing with dragonflies
A single metal slide
A tennis court of trouble

I remember the iron-on patches
Adventures in the woods
Cookies for sale
Clubhouse meetings

I remember the pad-mounted transformers
An eastern red cedar
A pink and white vanity
The treasured peanut butter cups

I remember the tulips
Red, orange, and yellow
The street light curfew
A bus stop of imagination

Ants

We fall in line.

Celebrating the ants we sing their songs.
Marching one by one,
our heads bob from side to side.
It's a game we love to play.

The game becomes routine,
so we are taught to be creative.
It's the same lesson plan for everyone,
yet the drawings all look different.

Propelling into conformity,
we dismiss our adolescence.
Gray now becomes the standard to track
progress and success.

We are monochromatic thinkers.
Expression cultivating an ailment,
yet told to be ourselves.
Confused by which ant to follow.

A battle begins as we search for an outlet,
Discovering new paths,
We now march alone.
The game is no longer a distraction.

We modernize the song in our heads.
Hiding the flamboyant melody,
we dismiss a single hued structure,
To the world we are bohemians.

Unreserved Learning

Shel Silverstein taught me how to be a dreamer
Henry King reminded me I simply can not last
Richard Evans taught me how to begin
Robert Frost guided me to choose the right path
Harper Lee taught my wings how to fly
John Scott warned me of the drums discordant
sound
Claude McKay taught me on how to fight
W H Davis convinced me to stand beneath the
boughs
In a little red book is where I kept all of these
lessons
The pages filled up with extravagant vows
I poured out my soul in black and blue ink
Each lesson an invitation that my heart would
allow

Obscure Glass

The clouds are pink today,
They almost look real

Yet when the windows fog,
I see the traces of your fingertips

Etched into my mind like an elaborate design,
Labeling me an astonishing creation

Longing for the approval of bystanders,
I'm waiting for the right moment

I stand watch as the story begins to bleed out

And as it goes, it drops
like those of a heavy rain pounding to the earth

no puddle to catch
no ocean to fall to

only the dust beneath the bystanders feet does it
bounce off of,
Leaving behind the mark of what is hidden

A design soon left to be forgotten

Still the clouds remain pink,
And none but I can recognize the fog

Jambienn P Roome

You brought me there first,
To the hill on lovers lane

We couldn't see stars,
But the cityscape welcomed us with open arms

We drove around with no destination,
You teaching me to never regret

Two teenagers walking through a graveyard,
Never more alive, but surrounded by death

Exchanging fantasies in a church parking lot,
We had our first kiss in that dragon filled park

While jumping the fence of a midnight pool,
Your camera flashed the beginning spark

At 14,000 feet I could feel my heart melt,
And with hair like sunshine,
back to the earth I fell.

Young and Naïve

He's everywhere
In everything I touch
Everything I see
It's him
He's inside of me
In the very first thought of the morning
In the very last before I go to sleep
My heart refuses to let go of the past
I'm dying inside
I can barely breathe
My mind keeps raining
Unsure of where to go
No matter where I run to
The signs are written with "no"
I'm becoming insane
Yet nothing has changed
Forever is a lie
The definition of pain
I'm told it will pass
This heartache of mine
But minutes feel like poison
And happiness a warning sign

Restless Guidance

If only I could travel back in time.
If only I could give myself one single piece of
advice.
I would say,

"let him go."

He wasn't the problem.
He wasn't to blame.
He couldn't be.

You see?

I was so wrapped up in the illusion of devotion,
that a picturesque affair suppressed my sound
mind and I became determined.

He would be mine.

I finally found myself feeling worthy of love.
His love.
I forgot about my own.

I never once thought of a time where we..

Wouldn't be..

"We"

Sure it sounds naïve, but that's exactly what I
was.
Clinging to the first lover I had ever known. I
wrote thirteen pages of a blossoming passion.

Never before had I ever written such beautiful
words.

Yet, they weren't about me.

I became obsessed with keeping the love I
worked so diligently to earn.
The color red was blinding me.
Brighter than any flame I had ever come across,
yet all I could acknowledge was the chocolate in
his eyes.

Chocolate, my new favorite color.

Soothing me.
Beckoning me.
Lying to me.

Whispering in my ear that I'd be safe forever,
while a voice was yelling at me to leave.

His voice.

How could such agonizing words escape the lips
of an angel? The angel that saved me from my
loneliness?
The angel who answered my prayers.
Prayers of me begging to have what everyone
else had.
Did I ask for too much?
Is this the repercussion of my impatience?
Of my begging?

No.
It couldn't be.
He doesn't mean it.

The fantasy I embraced so lovingly began to
crumble, so I chose to become chaos.
As hate consumed me, tears were all I had left.
I took those thirteen pages and I burned them.

I tore my own heart out and allowed the rest to
break.

Bits and pieces of me scattered everywhere I
went.

They were the parts of me that I kept locked
away so that no one could ever make me feel the
way he had.

The way I had.

I looked around at the pieces, but I could no
longer recognize me within them.

I became a ghost.

The most transparent version of myself
pretending to be happy, brought by the reflection
of a smile I thought to be believable.
My reassurances were all mechanical.

I was a lonely girl left to get up by myself with
no one to catch me when I fell.
Life had turned me into a nightmare and my
dreams were all deceiving me.

I could longer determine whether it was better to
be asleep or awake.
My mind's illusion deadened by a zombie-like
state.

I never saw that naive girl again.
I sometimes miss her determination.

But if given the decision,
Whether to go back or move forward,
I'd take that advice,
And save my heart from the torture.

My Inner Child

I tried to hide myself,
Yet somehow "hello" just kept coming

I tried to drown myself,
But the waves always washed her to shore

I tried to mute myself,
Yet the pain is what kept her screaming

I tried to deceive myself,
But that made her want to fight me more

I tried to forget myself,
Yet the moon declared her stunning

I tried to hate myself,
But her devotion wouldn't allow it anymore

Flowers for Zoe

I still have the picture saved
It was a sunny day in California
The kind of day described only in movies
Walking along the brick sidewalks
I saw it in the window

I pictured myself wearing it
Twirling around with flowers in my hair
Curls cascading down my shoulders
My something blue was everywhere

Nothing short of a fantasy
Spotlights of fireflies all perfectly timed
In a meadow worthy of fairies
I giggled out loud as if losing my mind

Toxic Fixation

What makes you feel safe?

Is it the fiery pit of chaos?

Is it the sound of whistling wind before the storm?

If everyone is smiling, do you feel the urge to run?

Do you count the seconds as if they will disappear before you get to first?

If your mind becomes quiet, do you fill the empty space?

If no worries are left, will you then create fear?

What world do you live in when yours is crumbling down?

Who could you possibly turn to if peace is finally found?

Delusion

I guess that I'm crazy..

I wrote a letter that will never get read
Imagined a love that will never exist
Painfully aware of the second hand ticking
I spend my days wishing that you were never
missed

I was waiting for you,
The Sunday afternoon that you passed
I was disappointed you weren't there
My confession prepared, if only you had asked

I'm jealous of those who knew you
I never got the chance
To the sounds of love and anxiety
My melancholy mind became trapped in a trance

With a new outlook on life
You helped slow the ticking down
One day I'll meet you in the heavens
And we'll be the talk of the town

Paralysis

I remember it all this time
The tapping at my leg
The familiarity of the figure leaning down
beside me
I forced my eyes to allow me to see through the
darkness
Catching a glimpse of her laying across me
I watched as the light from the tv made out the
tips of her ears
I pushed myself together
I found my way back

I Disagree

I'm told that hurt people always hurt people…
So why am I stuck in a cycle of repair?

Why is it that this loop always brings me to
those who need me?
Why is it never to myself?

How is it that my feet will not allow me to walk
away?
How is it that I'm the only one convincing them
to stay?

When did words begin to take the form of
knives?
When did I begin to fear voices when they are
raised?

Why do I wish upon stars for a love of dreams?
Why is it that I insist on giving all my love
away?

How can I long for a place I've never seen?
How can I miss a feeling a find cliche?

When did karma become a cruel form of
revenge?
When did heartbreak begin to leave me unfazed?

Why do I feel pain even when it isn't mine?
Why is it that when I break I'm never out of
time?

What do I have to do to end this cycle?
What is it that I can say to take the blame?

How is that I am always the one left hurting?
How is that the victim and the villain are one in
the same?

My Turn

I don't want to heal you
I don't want to play fix it anymore
I don't want to be needed
I don't want to smile and help you up
I don't want to make you happy
I don't want to listen
I don't want to force a laugh acting as if what
you say is a joke
I don't want to bite my tongue as you continue
to sing
I don't want to cheer you on
I don't want to hold you as you cry while I'm
breaking inside
I don't want to change my voice to sooth you
I don't want you to expect me to

I don't want to care
I don't want to wish you well
I don't want to feel bad about it

I don't want to share my love with you

I want it for MYSELF

I want to be selfish
I want to laugh at myself and pat my own back
I want to live out my dreams
I want to be all that I need
I want to check off my bucket list
I want my free time to be my own
I want to be happy
I want to feel whole
I want to sit on the beach and gaze at the stars
I want to stand at the top of mountains
I want to lay on the grass
I want to feel the leaves as they fall on my face
I want to sing my favorite song every morning I
wake
I want the whiskers of my cat brushing against
my cheek
I want to be loved
I want to be told it's okay

Healing

I feel myself getting better again

I scribble out a checklist
prepare for my goals
wake up with intention

My plan is quite perfect

I tell myself I'm content
Manifesting my dreams
Positivity won't fail me

I take my worries and transfer them to paper

I'm reflecting
I'm thankful
I'm forgetting what I had to do

Today is a good day

I have the support I need
Setting aside my troubles
Escaping by deciding to read

I feel better again

I am in sync with the sun
I have a new plan of action
I write a new checklist

I take a step back

A few panicking moments
Nothing can get me down
I'm starting over

I fall down a rabbit hole

Forgetting all color
My feet become roots
I can't seem to grow up

I'm hitting a wall

Consistency is key
I repeat that over and over
I've overcome my trauma

My memories attack me

I find my myself in awe
There's magic in the sky
I am finally in bloom

I'm surrounded by love

I'm building a home
Replacing the pictures and putting up shelves
I marvel at what I've created

I can no longer get up

My cat my only lifeline
I'm hurting through the mask
Disappointment is all that I've done

I discover motivation

The dark days are behind me
My inside voice screams
I press the reset button

I feel better again

Home

A place where lullabies always consist of a purr
A place where words pour out of your mind like
echos of a songbird
A place where the sun and the moon never say
goodbye
A place of such tranquility that no dictionary can
define
A place where your heart is full and love is in
the air you breathe
A place where the trees always sway to the
squirrels dancing feet
A place where the most heavenly sound always
greets you at the door
A place where nothing else matters,
Not anymore.

More

I look at these words
All of my reasons for tomorrow

Then I look at you

The pages keeping score
Over each and every little thing

I will always and forever

Love you

More.